COMMON CENTS, COMMON DREAMS

Peter J. Ferrara and
Michael D. Tanner

CATO
INSTITUTE
Washington, D.C.

Credits—

Cartoon on p. 24 reprinted by permission of Bob Gorrell and Creators Syndicate.

Cartoon on p. 48 reprinted by permission of the *Wichita Eagle*.

Cartoon on p. 51 reprinted by permission of Chuck Asay and Creators Syndicate.

ISBN: 1-882577-76-0

Printed in the United States of America.

Cato Institute
1000 Massachusetts Avenue, N.W.
Washington, D.C. 20001
www.cato.org

Contents

Introduction

We call this book *Common Cents, Common Dreams* because it is about how working men and women across this country can be freed to achieve the common dream of financial independence and security. Average and even low-income workers earn enough money to achieve substantial wealth by retirement. If they took the money that they currently pay in Social Security taxes and invested those funds in standard diversified portfolios of stocks and bonds, average-income families could expect to retire with accumulated savings of nearly $1 million or more. Even low-income workers could expect to save a half million dollars or more by retirement.

This book explains why and how that can be done. The key is for your congressional representatives to set you free to make your own choices about your own financial resources and future. Working men and women can achieve the results described above if they are allowed the freedom to choose a privately invested system structured for average, unsophisticated investors in place of Social Security.

That is no longer just a theory. Countries around the world are racing to set up such systems for their workers. As a result of one such system, in less than 10 years the average worker in the South American nation of Chile will have more savings and assets than the average American worker, even though Chilean workers earn only a small fraction of what American workers earn.

In this book, we will present calculations showing what today's workers will receive from Social Security and what they would receive from a privately invested system. Those calculations result from a private computer program produced by a team of economists and experts, assembled by the Cato Institute, in conjunction with the top accounting firm KPMG Peat Marwick. Later, we will tell you how you can access that program on the Internet and do such calculations for yourself.

1.
Jane's Challenge

Jane Everyman watched her six-year-old son Jack develop his skills at soccer practice. But her mind kept wandering to the problem of family finances. She and her husband, John, had never been rich, but they had always worked hard to provide a nice home and a comfortable life for their family. Still, there never seemed to be enough money to make ends meet.

John, 32, worked in construction. With his experience he had gained a position paying $36,000 a year. Jane, 30, had stopped working to stay home and take care of Jack and their four-year-old daughter Jill.

Sure, they had enough to keep food on the table and pay the essential bills. But Jane wanted to move out of the two-bedroom home they were renting and buy a little place of their own. That would require saving for a down payment. But, with monthly payments on their two used cars, occasional doctor's bills, and other basic expenses of raising a family, that would be difficult.

Jane planned to start working when Jill entered first grade in two years. She figured she could get a job at the mall like her friend Martha. The job paid $18,000 a year for about 35 hours per week, on a flexible work schedule.

With that, eventually they could save the down payment and meet the monthly mortgage. After a while, they might even be able to buy a new car and take a vacation once in a while. But still Jane wondered, would they ever be able to save enough money to get ahead?

She thought, too, about her father, George Franklin. He had worked most of his life as a supervisor for a small printing company. Without much education, he had managed to earn an average income throughout his career, through diligence and hard work. Whatever he saved, however, was used to send Jane's brother Ben to college and to pay for the uncovered medical bills of his wife, Elizabeth, Jane's mother. Elizabeth died last year after a long illness.

Her father's shop didn't have a pension plan, but her dad figured he could rely on Social Security. When he retired this year, however, he was shocked to learn that Social Security would pay only $935.50 per month, which is the average monthly benefit from Social Security. He was also shocked to discover that if he went back to work to earn some extra money, the government would reduce his Social Security benefits $1 for every $3 he earned over $13,500 for the year. He would also have to pay Social Security taxes on his earnings, in addition to federal and state income taxes. As a result, he would lose two-thirds or more of any earnings over $13,500 per year to taxes and lost Social Security benefits. Moreover, if he earned more than $19,400 for the year in non-Social Security income, his Social Security benefits would be subject to federal and state income taxes. That would leave him with almost no net gain for any earnings above $13,500 per year.

Jane wondered how her family could avoid that trap. But besides saving for their new home, soon they would have to start setting aside college funds for Jack and Jill. How could they save for retirement too?

John was no financial wizard; he spent his time watching ESPN, not *Wall Street Week*. So Jane turned to her brother Ben, who was an economist. Ben pointed out to Jane the money her family was paying in payroll taxes for Social Security. The government charged John 6.2 percent of his wages for Social Security, or a total of $2,232 for the year. The government charged John another 1.45 percent for Medicare, or $522 for the year. Together, John's payroll taxes totaled $2,754 for the year (for an example, see Figure 1.1).

But that was just the beginning. John's employer had to match those amounts, paying another $2,754 for John. Ben told Jane, "That's not charity from the employer. John's company just takes that money out of the wages it would otherwise pay him. His salary is $2,754 lower than it would be if the company didn't have to pay those taxes." So John effectively bears the entire tax, or $5,508 per year.

That was not all. Ben also noted that if Jane worked at the mall for $18,000 a year, she and her employer together would pay Social Security payroll taxes of $2,232 for the year, plus another $522 for Medicare, for a total of $2,754. At that point, total annual payroll taxes from Jane, her husband, and their employers would be $8,262.

Jane was outraged. That was more than they could ever hope to save in a year. Ben suggested that their hard-earned money—money they could use for their retirement and other needs—was going to Social Security.

Considering that Social Security was already paying her father so little, Jane wondered what she and John would get back for all their money. She had read news reports about Social Security's going bankrupt after the baby-boom generation retired. What would happen to her and John?

Jane's thoughts returned to the soccer field, where Jack outraced his friends to the ball and scored a goal. She wondered about Jack and Jill's future. If Social Security taxes were already so high for her and John, what would her children's taxes be? And if Social Security went bankrupt before she and John retired, what would be left for Jack and Jill? What could they expect in return for their huge tax payments?

And what about her father? She knew that he needed his benefits and that he already received too little. Was there any way out of this mess?

Figure 1.1
TYPICAL PAY SUMMARY

PAY SUMMARY		
Employee: Richard Roe		
SSN: 000-00-0000		
Pay Period: 5/1/98–5/14/98		

1. Estimated payroll allocation:	$1026.59
2. Government cost: tax administration (est.):	15.43
3. Government cost: mandated program admin. (est.):	4.25
4. Government tax: unemployment insurance (est.):	10.66
5. Government tax: workers' compensation (est.):	9.46
6. Government tax: Social Security, employer's	
share:	**56.83**
7. Government tax: Medicare, employer's share:	13.29
Gross pay:	**$916.67**
8. Government tax: federal income tax:	105.00
9. Government tax: state income tax:	36.45
10. Government tax: Social Security, employee's	
share:	**56.83**
11. Government tax: Medicare, employee's share:	13.29
12. Government tax: city income tax:	18.43
Net pay:	**$686.67**

2.
Losing a Fortune

When Congress passed Social Security in 1935, a House committee stated in its report on the bill, ''We can't ask support for a plan [that is] not at least as good as any American could buy from a private insurance company. The very least a citizen should expect is to get his money back upon retirement.''

But Jane Everyman began to doubt that that was true for her family. Her doubt hardened last month when her husband's friend Carlos Bolivar came to visit from the South American country of Chile.

Carlos told Jane about a new system his country had adopted in 1981. Instead of paying into social security, Chileans pay into a personal investment and insurance account. The money is invested in real stocks and bonds over the years, and private insurance covers their survivors' and disability benefits.

Like John, Carlos worked in construction. But, because Chile is a poorer country, Carlos earned only $12,000 per year in U.S. dollars, one-third of what John made in the United States. Still, after paying into the private system for 15 years, Carlos had accumulated $41,939. He showed Jane the sum in his personal passbook where he kept track of his retirement funds.

Hearing this, Jane thought she could only dream of the day when she and John could save more than $40,000.

Jane was even more shocked when she heard a few days later about someone doing that here in the United States. Her brother Ben told her about his brother-in-law Pat Garrett, now a county sheriff in Texas. Pat's county opted out of Social Security for its employees in 1981, just before the law was changed to prohibit that in the future. The county set up a private system much like that in many South American countries. Workers and their county employers pay into an individual private investment account for each worker. A major investment company picks the stocks and bonds for each worker's account. The system also provides workers with private life insurance to cover survivors' benefits and private disability insurance to cover disability benefits.

Pat makes $36,000 a year, just like John, after starting out 15 years ago at $22,000. After paying into the private system for 15 years, Pat has accumulated $95,338.

John and Jane's Prospects

Jane began to wonder how she and John would do under such a system and how it would compare with Social Security. She asked Ben if he would help her.

First, Ben calculated future Social Security benefits for her and John. If John continued to receive standard raises over the years, Social Security would pay him $1,341 per month when he retired. If Jane did not go back to work, then Social Security would pay an additional $671 per month for her, for a total of $2,012 per month, or $24,144 for the year.[1] That would be in 2032, when John would be ready to retire.

What if John's tax payments had been saved and invested in the private sector instead? Ben calculated that under three alternative investment strategies. One strategy was to invest in a mutual fund holding a broad range of stocks. A second strategy was to invest in a mutual fund holding a broad range of bonds. A third strategy was to invest in a mixed mutual fund, with half the money in stocks and half in bonds.

---

[1]All figures are in 1997 dollars unless otherwise noted.

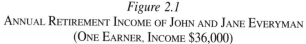

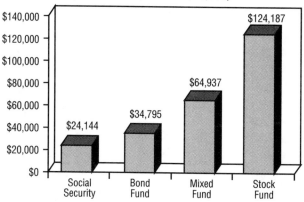

Figure 2.1
ANNUAL RETIREMENT INCOME OF JOHN AND JANE EVERYMAN
(ONE EARNER, INCOME $36,000)

Over the past 70 years, stocks on the New York Stock Exchange have earned an average real return of 7 percent after inflation. Stocks of smaller companies and foreign stocks have averaged even more. So Ben conservatively estimated that the stock mutual fund would, on average, earn a 7 percent real (after inflation) return. Corporate bonds over the past 70 years have earned an average real return of 3 percent after inflation. Ben estimated that the bond mutual fund would earn a 3 percent real return, on average, for John and Jane. Finally, Ben assumed the mixed stock and bond mutual fund would fall in the middle with a real return of 5 percent.

The results are shown in Figure 2.1. If John and Jane invested the funds John and his employer would otherwise pay into Social Security during John's entire career, then with the mixed stock and bond mutual fund they would retire with a personal retirement account of $727,971 in 1997 dollars. That fund would finance an annuity paying them $64,937 each year, or almost 3 times the amount that Social Security would pay.

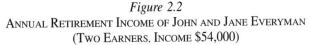

Figure 2.2
ANNUAL RETIREMENT INCOME OF JOHN AND JANE EVERYMAN
(TWO EARNERS, INCOME $54,000)

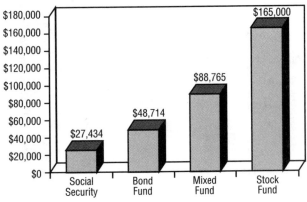

If they invested in the stock mutual fund, John and Jane would retire with a total investment account of $1,228,245 in 1997 dollars. That fund would finance an annuity paying $124,187 each year, more than five times what Social Security would pay. Investing in the bond mutual fund would yield total retirement assets of $446,317, which would pay $34,795 a year, or 44 percent more than Social Security.

Now suppose Jane went back to work in two years as she planned, earning $18,000 per year with standard raises every year. At retirement, Social Security would pay them a combined total of $2,286 per month, or $27,434 for the year. That would be only $3,290 more per year than they would receive had Jane not worked at all. That is all John and Jane would get from Social Security tax payments by Jane and her employer of $2,232 per year, rising with Jane's salary over the years.

What if they both could invest in the private system instead? As Figure 2.2 shows, investing in the mixed stock and bond mutual fund would give them nearly $1 million at retirement. That fund would finance an annuity paying them almost

$90,000 per year, or well over three times what Social Security would pay. With the stock mutual fund, John and Jane would retire with a balance of $1,640,767. That account would pay them about $165,000 per year, or about six times what Social Security would pay. With the bond mutual fund, the investment account would reach $624,855, paying $48,714 per year, almost twice what Social Security would pay.

The Salesman and the School Teacher

Jane was so excited about what she had learned that she told her friends about it. The following week she was talking to her neighbor LaShawn Jefferson, who had recently moved into the house next door with her husband Tom. LaShawn and Tom were both 26 years old. They met in college and were married after graduation. Today Tom is a salesman for the Independence Paper Company. He makes $32,000 per year, which is about the median earnings for a full-time male worker in the United States. LaShawn is a school teacher. She earns $26,000 per year, which is about the median earnings for a full-time female worker in the United States.

LaShawn was very interested in what Jane told her. She asked Jane if Ben would calculate how she and Tom would do in the private system compared with Social Security. Ben was glad to do it.

Ben assumed that Tom and LaShawn would receive standard salary increases throughout their careers, which would keep them at the median income for full-time male and female workers each year. He also assumed that they would invest in the private system the amount that they and their employers would otherwise pay into Social Security. As Figure 2.3 shows, Ben found that if they invested in the mixed stock and bond fund, they would retire with a total combined amount of $1,181,565, in 1997 dollars. That fund would finance an annuity paying them $105,398 per year in today's dollars, almost three times what Social Security would pay. Figure 2.3 shows the results of the various investment strategies.

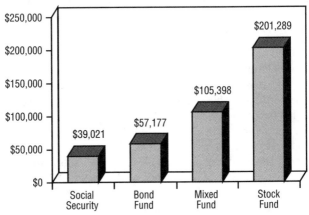

Figure 2.3
ANNUAL RETIREMENT INCOME OF
TOM AND LASHAWN JEFFERSON
(TWO EARNERS, INCOME $58,000)

The Waitress and the Mechanic

Still, LaShawn worried about how lower-income people would do. After all, the government had established the system with them in mind.

For example, what about Mary Revere, the 22-year-old waitress at the restaurant where LaShawn and Jane often ate lunch? Mary earned just $15,000 a year. Surely Social Security was a good deal for her? But Figure 2.4 shows that, again with just standard raises over her career, Mary would retire with a total accumulated fund of $321,788 if she paid into a mixed stock and bond fund instead of Social Security. That fund would pay her $28,704 per year in retirement, more than double what Social Security would.

Mary's boyfriend was a 24-year-old auto mechanic named Paul, who earned $20,000 per year. As Figure 2.5 demonstrates, if they married and then invested in a mixed stock and bond fund earning standard returns, they would retire with a

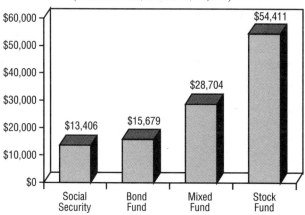

Figure 2.4
ANNUAL RETIREMENT INCOME OF MARY REVERE
(ONE EARNER, INCOME $15,000)

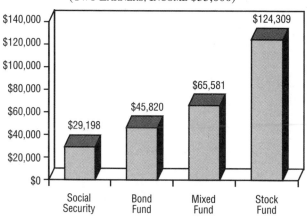

Figure 2.5
ANNUAL RETIREMENT INCOME OF MARY AND PAUL
(TWO EARNERS, INCOME $35,000)

total combined investment fund of about $750,000. That fund would pay them $65,581 per year in today's dollars, more than double what Social Security would pay.

Jane's Conclusion

After getting the facts, Jane realized that the issue over Social Security was not just whether or when it would go bankrupt. Working people were losing money every day they were forced to participate in the system without a private option. Over their lives, they and other middle-income couples like them would lose nearly $1 million each, and their children would lose even more.

3.
Why Social Security Is a Bad Deal for Today's Workers

As Jane found out, Social Security is a bad deal for today's workers. Those workers would get much higher returns and benefits if they were allowed to invest in the private sector. That would be true even if Social Security were able to pay its promised benefits in the future, which is highly unlikely. (We'll discuss that more in the next chapter.)

Many people believe that the money they pay in Social Security taxes is put away in Washington to pay for their retirement. But that is not so. The type of Social Security system that we currently have in the United States is called a pay-as-you-go system. The money that you pay into Social Security is not saved and invested for your future retirement benefits. Instead, it is immediately used to pay Social Security benefits for today's retirees. Social Security expects to pay your future benefits with taxes collected from your children and grandchildren.

Social Security never makes any real capital investments in the private sector the way a private retirement system would. Consequently, Social Security never earns the full market rate of return on collected taxes.

In many ways Social Security resembles the type of pyramid or Ponzi scheme that is illegal in all 50 states. Individuals at the top of the pyramid receive a very good rate of return.

For example, people who retired in the early years of the program paid very low payroll taxes, and some paid taxes for only a few years before retirement. Yet they received benefits many times greater than the taxes they paid, supported by the taxes of other workers. But the workers later in the chain do not do as well.

The Ponzi Scheme

Why is Social Security often called a Ponzi scheme? Charles Ponzi, an Italian immigrant, started the first such scheme in Boston in 1916. He convinced some people to allow him to invest their money, but he never made any real investments. He just took the money from later investors and gave it to the earlier investors, paying them a handsome profit on what they originally paid in. He then used the early investors as advertisements to get more investors, using their money to pay a profit to previous investors, and so on.

To keep paying a profit to previous investors, Ponzi had to continue to find more and more new investors. Eventually, he couldn't expand the number of new investors fast enough and the system collapsed. Because he never made any real investments, he had no funds to pay back the newer investors. They lost all the money they "invested" with Ponzi.

Ponzi was convicted of fraud and sent to prison for two years. When he came out, he returned to Italy, where he became a top economic adviser to Benito Mussolini.

But Ponzi's scheme lives on today in the majesty of the Social Security system. Just like Ponzi's plan, Social Security does not make any real investments—it just takes money from the later "investors," or taxpayers, to pay benefits to the earlier, now retired, taxpayers. Like Ponzi, Social Security will not be able to recruit new "investors" fast enough to continue paying promised benefits to previous investors. Because each year there are fewer young workers relative to the number of retirees, Social Security will eventually collapse just like Ponzi's scheme.

The first regular Social Security recipient, Ida Mae Fuller of Vermont, illustrates that point. Ms. Fuller paid Social Security taxes for only three years before she retired in 1940. By that time she and her employer had paid a total of only $44 in Social Security taxes. Nevertheless, Fuller collected Social Security retirement benefits for the next 35 years until she died in 1975 at the age of 100. During that period she received $20,993.52 in benefits. Though not much money in itself, it was an enormous return on the taxes she and her employer had paid into the program.

But over time, payroll taxes rose and workers paid more and more for longer periods of time. As Figure 3.1 shows, the payroll tax has been raised 38 times since Social Security was enacted. As a result, workers have received less and less of a good deal from the program.

Eventually, workers who had paid into the system for their entire careers began to retire. Those workers no longer had the windfall advantage of those who had retired in Social Security's early years. They and all future workers were now stuck in a pay-as-you-go system that made no real capital investment for them. As a result, they lost the much higher returns and benefits they could have received through a privately invested system.

Workers who had paid Social Security taxes for their entire careers did not begin to retire until the early 1980s. By then, those retirees would have done better had they saved and invested privately. Even those retirees, however, avoided the sharp Social Security tax increases of the 1960s, 1970s, and early 1980s for a large part of their careers. Today's young workers who are in their 20s and 30s will get the worst deal; they will pay those increased taxes for their entire careers. Many will actually receive a negative return from Social Security—less money back in benefits than they paid in taxes. They will actually lose money on their investment!

Women, the Poor, and Minorities

Because of those problems, Social Security has now become a bad deal for all of today's workers—high-income

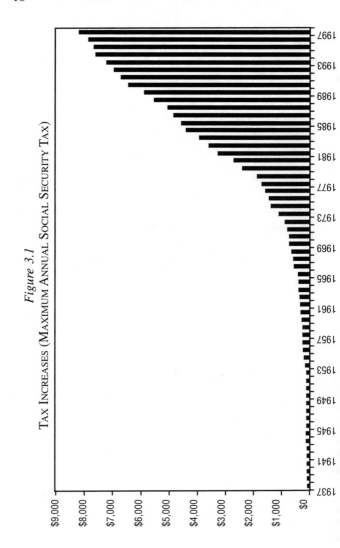

Figure 3.1
TAX INCREASES (MAXIMUM ANNUAL SOCIAL SECURITY TAX)

and low-income, married and single, big families and small, men and women. Everyone would have a much more secure retirement through a privately invested system. But some groups, especially women, the poor, and minorities, get a particularly bad deal from Social Security and would gain the most from a new system that allowed private investment.

Social Security was designed at a time when most women did not work. As a result, it provided special subsidies for nonworking spouses. But the family today is much different from the family of the 1930s. Most women work. As a result, Social Security has become extremely unfair to women. For example, under the current system a wife automatically receives Social Security benefits equal to at least half of her husband's benefits. A working woman receives nothing in return for her lifetime of Social Security taxes unless she earns benefits greater than 50 percent of those her husband receives. That unfairly penalizes millions of women who work only part-time or in low-wage jobs.

In a privately invested system, by contrast, a working woman would receive benefits based on every dollar that she contributed to her account. Because of the higher returns under a privately invested system, both she and her husband would receive far higher retirement incomes than they would under Social Security.

Of all those penalized by our current Social Security system, perhaps the working poor suffer most. First, the Social Security payroll tax is an extremely regressive tax. Because the amount of income subject to the tax is capped, low-income people pay a much higher percentage of their income than do wealthier workers. Moreover, the payroll tax is a tax only on wages. Income from capital gains, interest, and other investments is exempt from the tax. Thus, the burden of financing Social Security falls primarily on middle- and low-income Americans.

At the same time, Social Security benefits disproportionately go to higher-income workers. While yearly benefits are determined by a progressive formula designed to benefit low-wage workers, the total amount a person receives in lifetime

Social Security benefits depends, not surprisingly, on how long he or she lives. A person who dies at age 66 receives relatively few benefits. Someone who lives to be 100 collects far more. Unfortunately, for many reasons the poor tend to die much earlier than the wealthy. Several studies, including one by the prestigious RAND Corporation, have found that, as a result, Social Security acts like a reverse Robin Hood, taking from the poor and giving to the rich.

In a privately invested system, however, benefits do not depend on how long you live. The benefits you receive are based on what you pay into the system plus the return that your investments have earned. Moreover, you have a property right to the money in your account. You own that money. If you die early, the money becomes part of your estate and your heirs will inherit it.

In contrast, the U.S. Supreme Court has ruled that you have *no* contractual or property right to Social Security benefits, no matter how much you've paid in taxes. Congress can take some or all of your benefits away at any time.

Nestor v. Fleming

Many people believe that Social Security is an "earned right." That is, because they have paid Social Security taxes they are entitled to receive Social Security benefits. The government encourages that belief by referring to Social Security taxes as "contributions" as in the Federal Insurance Contribution Act. However, in the 1960 case of *Fleming v. Nestor*, the U.S. Supreme Court ruled that workers have no legally binding contractual rights to their Social Security benefits, and those benefits can be cut or even eliminated at any time.

Ephram Nestor was a Bulgarian immigrant who came to the United States in 1918 and paid Social Security taxes from 1936, the year the system began operating, until he retired in 1955. A year after he retired, Nestor was deported for having been a member of the Communist Party in the

1930s. In 1954 Congress had passed a law saying that any person deported from the United States should lose their Social Security benefits. Accordingly, Nestor's $55.60 per month Social Security checks were stopped. Nestor sued, claiming that because he had paid Social Security taxes he had a right to Social Security benefits.

The Supreme Court disagreed, saying, "To engraft upon the Social Security system a concept of 'accrued property rights' would deprive it of the flexibility and boldness in adjustment to ever changing conditions which it demands." The Court went on to say, "It is apparent that the non-contractual interest of an employee covered by the [Social Security] Act cannot be soundly analogized to that of the holder of an annuity, whose right to benefits is bottomed on his contractual premium payments."

The Court's decision was not surprising. In an earlier case, *Helvering v. Davis* (1937), the Court had ruled that Social Security was *not* a contributory insurance program, saying, "The proceeds of both the employee and employer taxes are to be paid into the Treasury like any other internal revenue generally, and are not earmarked in any way."

Therefore, your Social Security benefits are always subject to the whim of politicians in Washington. Indeed, many proposals to cut Social Security benefits are currently being debated.

In contrast, under a privatized Social Security system, workers would have full property rights in their retirement accounts. They would own their accounts and the money in them, the same way people own their IRA or 401(k) plan.

Second, lower-income workers tend to start work at an earlier age than higher-income workers. Lower-income workers often begin working right out of high school, whereas higher-income workers are more likely to begin working after college or graduate school. Social Security generally gives workers no credit for their early years of work because it counts only the 35 years of highest earnings in calculating benefits. The taxes paid during those early work years are simply lost.

In a privately invested system, however, every dollar you contribute to your account is yours. And those early contributions can be worth a great deal—$1,000 invested in a stock fund at age 18 would be worth $32,000 at retirement (given historic rates of market return).

Third, low-income workers have less savings and are less likely to have corporate pensions than higher-wage earners. In fact, the poorest 20 percent of the elderly depend on Social Security for 81 percent of their income, while Social Security provides only 20 percent of the income of the wealthiest 20 percent of retirees. The poorest 20 percent are the workers who would benefit most from the higher returns of a privately invested system.

Remember Mary Revere, the waitress earning only $15,000 per year. As shown in Figure 2.4, with a mixed stock and bond fund instead of Social Security, she would retire with an accumulated retirement account of $321,788, which would pay more than twice as much as Social Security. With a stock fund, she would retire with more than $500,000, which would pay her about four times as much as Social Security.

Moreover, if she married her boyfriend Paul (the 24-year-old auto mechanic making $23,000 per year), a mixed stock and bond fund would let them retire with a combined investment account of about $750,000. That fund would pay three times what Social Security promises them. With a stock fund, that low-income couple would retire with a combined investment fund of almost $1.25 million in today's dollars, which would pay them more than four times as much as Social Security.

In addition, low-income workers will be hurt the most by the higher taxes and reduced benefits that will be necessary to solve the current Social Security system's financial crisis. Low-income workers cannot afford to pay higher taxes while they are working, nor can they afford to receive lower benefits in retirement. With the privately invested system, they could avoid the whole problem.

Social Security is particularly unfair to African-Americans and other minorities. African-Americans can expect to live far fewer years in retirement than can whites because of their lower life expectancy. For example, the life expectancy of a black man today is just 65 years and 6 months. Millions of black men will pay Social Security taxes their entire lives and never receive a dime in benefits. At the same time, black seniors who do reach retirement are far more likely than others to be dependent on Social Security for almost all of their income.

How the Traditional Family Loses

As indicated above, Social Security was designed in the 1930s with the "traditional" family in mind. At that time, it was assumed that the husband worked and the wife stayed home to care for the children. But Social Security has now become terribly unfair for those families as well.

Remember the case of John and Jane. In Chapter 2, we saw what would happen if John worked and earned $36,000 per year while Jane stayed home to care for the children. Paying into a private mixed stock and bond fund instead of Social Security, they would retire with almost $750,000 in today's dollars, which would pay them almost three times what Social Security would. With a stock mutual fund, they would retire with almost $1.25 million in today's dollars, which would pay them more than five times what Social Security would pay.

Moreover, the private system keeps the money in the family. Retirees can choose to leave some or even most of their saved funds to their children and grandchildren and still receive significantly higher benefits than Social Security would pay. Such funds could help the retiree's children finance a new home or start a new business, or help the grandchildren go to college, law school, or medical school.

With financial resources kept within the family and its members helping each other, the family tends to stay close and work together. By contrast, with the government taking money out of the family and paying benefits through Social Security, the family is more likely to drift apart, as often happens when government takes over the family's role. The children figure the government is supposed to take care of their parents. The parents have far less with which to help their children and grandchildren, who then go off to pursue their own dreams and aspirations. That is why allowing workers a private alternative to Social Security would be profoundly pro-family.

Social Security and Economic Growth

Finally, Social Security is a bad deal for today's workers because it deprives them of the broader benefits to the national economy that would result from a privately invested system. Such a system would likely substantially increase national savings and investment, with hundreds of billions in additional dollars pouring into the capital markets each year. That would create new jobs and expand economic opportunity. It would increase wages, since higher capital investment increases productivity, which in turn results in higher wages. Lower payroll taxes resulting from the private system would also increase jobs and take-home pay. Social Security is bad for all workers because it deprives them of those general economic benefits. But more jobs, higher wages, and other economic gains would be most valuable for lower-income workers.

Check It Out Yourself

How does Social Security compare with what you could earn from private investment? You can check it out for yourself. If you have access to the Internet, you can contact the Cato Institute's Social Security Web site at www. socialsecurity.org. In addition to materials on Social Security privatization, this site contains an interactive calculator designed by the accounting firm of KPMG Peat Marwick. You can enter your personal data (age, income, etc.) and see what your future Social Security benefits would be and how they compare with what you could earn in a privately invested system.

"We revised the way we calculate Social Security payments....You're due back at work next Tuesday!"

4.
The Coming Collapse of Social Security

According to a famous poll, almost twice as many young adults believe in UFOs as believe Social Security will still exist when they retire. Although we cannot vouch for their view of extraterrestrial life, those young people are not far off in their estimation of Social Security's future.

In 2013, less than 15 years from now, the Social Security system will begin to run a deficit; that is, it will begin to spend more on benefits than it brings in through taxes (see Figure 4.1).

Figure 4.1
FUTURE FINANCIAL CRISIS
SOCIAL SECURITY REVENUE VS. COST OF BENEFITS

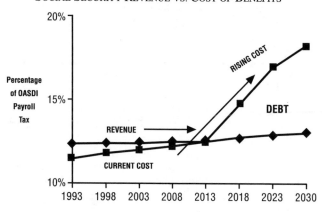

Anyone who has ever run a business or balanced a checkbook understands that when you are spending more than you bring in, something has to give—you need either to earn more money or to spend less to keep things balanced. For Social Security, that means either higher taxes or lower benefits.

In theory, Social Security is supposed to continue paying benefits after 2013 by drawing on the Social Security Trust Fund. That trust fund is supposed to provide enough money to guarantee benefits until 2032, when it will be exhausted. But one of Washington's dirty little secrets is that there really isn't a trust fund. The government spent that money long ago to finance general government spending and to hide the true size of the federal budget deficit. The trust fund now consists only of IOUs—promises that sometime in the future the government will replace that money, which can be done only by collecting more taxes.

The Trust Fund Fraud

What is the Social Security Trust Fund? Ever since the last set of Social Security reforms in 1983, Social Security has run a surplus; that is, Social Security taxes have brought in more revenue than is necessary to pay current benefits. The surplus will continue until 2013, when the situation will reverse and Social Security will begin to run a deficit. The present surplus is lent to the federal government in return for specially issued government bonds. The government then uses those borrowed surplus funds to finance its general operations, from roads and bridges to welfare and foreign aid.

About half of the trust fund consists of those bonds. The other half consists of an accounting entry that "attributes" interest to the bonds. But there is no actual money in the so-called trust fund. To pay benefits out of the trust fund, the government will have to redeem the bonds and pay the actual interest. But because no money has been set aside for that purpose, the government will have to find the money somewhere else, for example, by raising taxes.

Most of us are accustomed to thinking of a trust fund as an asset. That's what it would be if we had one. But in the case of Social Security, the trust fund is really a liability—money the government owes future retirees.

The trust fund is actually irrelevant to Social Security's future. Consider what would happen if the trust fund had never existed. In 2013, when Social Security begins to run a deficit, the government would have to raise taxes in order to pay all the promised benefits. And what happens to the trust fund? In 2013, the government will have to redeem its bonds in order to pay promised benefits. To redeem the bonds, it will have to raise taxes. Either way, today's young workers can expect a massive tax increase.

If Social Security is going to continue to pay the benefits it has promised, a huge tax increase on young workers will be necessary. How large? Paying all the promised future retirement benefits would require raising the payroll tax from the current level of 12.4 percent to nearly 18 percent. This does not even include the Medicare portion of the payroll tax, which is 2.9 percent today. Medicare is in such bad shape that paying all the benefits promised under both Medicare and Social Security would require raising the total payroll tax from today's 15.3 percent to nearly 28 percent—almost doubling that tax!

Even that estimate may be too optimistic. Those figures are based on the ''intermediate'' projections of Social Security's Board of Trustees. As A. Haeworth Robertson, former chief actuary at the Social Security Administration, has noted, however, those projections have been wrong more often than not. In fact, in the past 10 years the trustees have had to move forward Social Security's projected insolvency date six times.

Historically, the trustees' ''pessimistic'' projections have been closer to the mark, Robertson has pointed out. Under those projections, two things happen. First, the date that Social Security begins to run a deficit moves to 2006, just a few years from now. Second, the payroll tax necessary to meet all the promised benefits under Social Security would have to increase to 24 percent. If Medicare were included, the total payroll tax would have to be as high as 44 percent, nearly triple what it is today. That is why Professor Lawrence Kotlikoff of Boston University has estimated that the total tax burden (both payroll taxes and income taxes) on a child born today could exceed 82 percent of his income during his working lifetime.

The main reason for Social Security's financial crisis is simple demographics—the graying of the American population. As we saw in the last chapter, Social Security is a pay-as-you-go system that requires more and more workers to pay into the system to support each retiree. But exactly the opposite is happening; the retiree population is growing larger relative to the working population.

The most well-known reason for that is the baby-boom generation, born during a period of high fertility in the United States from the late 1940s to the early 1960s. Between 2010 and 2015, that generation will start to retire, causing Social Security benefit expenditures to explode.

Another demographic development has made the problem even worse. Starting in the early 1960s, after development of birth control pills, birth rates in the United States, as well as in the rest of the Western world, declined sharply. Today, the fertility rate, or lifetime births per woman, is about 2.1, roughly the level necessary to keep the U.S. population from declining.

Thus, the baby boom was followed by a baby bust. As a result, when the baby-boom generation retires and causes benefit expenditures to explode, the generation of workers behind it, who are supposed to finance its retirement benefits out of current taxes in the pay-as-you-go system, will be relatively small. Incoming taxes during the initial baby-boom retirement era will consequently fall short of benefits by an even wider margin.

Still another demographic development is exacerbating the problem. Americans are living longer and, given high-tech medical advances already under way in genetics, biotechnology, and other fields, the potential for much longer life expectancy in the 21st century is great. As a result, Social Security expenditures will rocket even further past available revenues.

Figure 4.2
WORKERS PER SOCIAL SECURITY BENEFICIARY

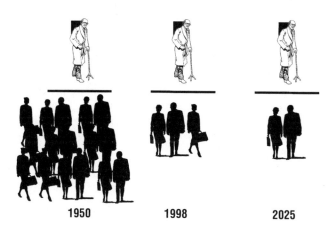

| 1950 | 1998 | 2025 |

The impact of those demographic developments can be seen in the declining ratio of workers to retirees, as shown in Figure 4.2. In 1950, 16 workers were paying into Social Security for every retiree drawing benefits, a strong foundation for a pay-as-you-go system. Today, 3.3 workers are paying for every retiree receiving benefits. By the time today's young workers retire, even under the intermediate projections there will be only 2 workers for every retiree, and the number will fall to fewer than 2 after that. With only about 60 percent as many workers per retiree as today, future payroll tax revenues would be sufficient to cover only about 60 percent of promised benefits. That alone would require an increase in tax rates of about two-thirds to cover promised benefits.

Moreover, under the pessimistic projections, the ratio of workers to retirees will fall below 2 before today's young workers retire and decline to 1.5 in 2050 when they will still be drawing benefits. That drop of more than 50 percent in the worker/retiree ratio means revenues would cover less than half of promised benefits. Payroll tax rates would then have to more than double on that score alone to meet promised benefits.

Still another factor is worsening the problem. The rate of growth has slowed significantly over the past 25 to 30 years, which means less in payroll taxes generated by those wages, unless tax rates are increased.

The gap between Social Security's funds and its future obligations is huge—as much as $9 trillion. In contrast, our national debt is only $5.4 trillion. Clearly, the Social Security system cannot continue on its current course. Nor can it be fixed through small, incremental changes such as raising taxes or cutting benefits. We need a totally new system that is not vulnerable to changing demographics.

5.
The Worldwide Revolution in Social Security

America's Social Security crisis is not unique. Around the globe, government retirement systems are encountering similar demographic and financial problems. From South America to Great Britain, from Southeast Asia to Eastern Europe, countries are already changing their systems to allow their workers to gain the advantage of a privately invested system. Even China is setting up a "privatized" social security system based on individually owned, privately invested accounts. If America doesn't change, we will be left behind.

Chile
The remarkable political turnaround for social security systems began with the South American nation of Chile, which adopted a private option for its social security system in 1981. Chile was the first country in the Western Hemisphere to adopt a social security system; it did so in 1925, 10 years before the United States. By 1981 the Chilean system had many of the same problems our system faces today. Payroll taxes were higher than 26 percent, yet the system still ran deficits that drained the federal budget. Long-range projections showed the program's financial gaps widening further. Benefits were inadequate and far below what workers could have earned by saving and investing in the private sector.

Chile's private-sector reforms were developed by a group of young, American-educated Chilean economists, led by Labor and Social Security Secretary José Piñera. Rather than postpone problems with Chile's social security system through tax increases or benefit cuts, they developed a completely new system based on individually owned, privately invested retirement accounts called Pension Savings Accounts (PSAs).

Under Chile's PSA system, neither workers nor employers pay a social security tax to the state, nor does the worker collect a government-funded pension. Instead, during working years, the employer automatically deposits 10 percent of each worker's wages into the worker's individual PSA. Workers may, if they choose, contribute an additional 10 percent of their wages (over the minimum required 10 percent) on a tax-free basis (like an American individual retirement account). Generally, workers will contribute more than 10 percent of their salaries if they want to retire early or obtain higher pensions.

Workers choose one of about 14 private, expert investment companies approved by the government to manage their PSAs. Those companies choose the stocks, bonds, and other investments for the workers' accounts, subject to government regulation prohibiting high-risk investments. As a result, workers do not have to be experienced investors to participate in the private system.

Workers are free to change from one management company to another. For that reason, companies compete strenuously to provide a higher return on investment, better customer service, and lower administrative fees. Workers are given PSA passbooks and every three months receive a statement informing them of how much money has accumulated in their retirement accounts and how well their investment funds have performed. The accounts bear the workers' names and are their property.

At retirement, workers can use the accumulated funds in their individual pension accounts to buy an annuity from any private insurance company. The annuity pays a specified monthly income, indexed to inflation, for the life of the worker. The annuity also pays survivors' benefits for the retiree's spouse or other dependents after the worker dies.

Alternatively, instead of buying an annuity, retirees may leave the funds in their PSAs and make regular withdrawals, subject to limits based on the life expectancy of the retirees and their dependents. When a worker dies, the funds remaining in the account can be left to a spouse, children, or other heirs.

The reform was designed so that, with normal investment returns, workers contributing the required amounts each year would receive retirement benefits equal to 80 percent of their final salaries. That is about double the replacement rate of the U.S. Social Security system, which pays about 42 percent of preretirement income for average income workers. In fact, investment returns under the private system in Chile have been much higher than expected, which has resulted in even greater benefits for workers.

The government also guarantees a minimum retirement benefit for all workers. If a retiree's private benefits fall below a minimum level for any reason, the government pays additional benefits to the retiree to bring total benefits up to the minimum guaranteed level. The minimum benefit is equal to 40 percent of average wages, which is about what the U.S. Social Security system pays to average-income workers.

In contrast to company-based private pension systems, which generally impose costs on workers who leave before a given number of years and which sometimes go bankrupt—thus depriving workers of both their jobs and their pension rights—the PSA system is completely independent of the company employing the worker. Since the PSA is tied to the worker, not the company where he works, the account is fully portable. Workers aren't ''locked into'' jobs by pension arrangements.

The retirement age under the new system is 65 for men and 60 for women, but workers can retire earlier if they have accumulated sufficient funds to provide a minimum level of benefits. Workers can speed up their accumulation of funds and retire even earlier by making voluntary extra contributions during working years or earning higher-than-expected returns. Workers can continue to work after retirement as much as they choose without being required to contribute to the retirement system.

Workers in the private system also contribute an additional 3 percent of wages for private life and disability insurance, as well as for administration of their accounts. The insurance replaces the survivors' and disability benefits paid by the old system for disability or death occurring during the preretirement years of the worker. The entire private system is indexed for inflation.

Workers who were already in the workforce at the time of the reform had, of course, paid taxes into the old system for several years. The government issued to those who chose to switch to the new private system special bonds, called recognition bonds, to compensate them for their past taxes. Workers hold the bonds in their PSAs. The amount of the bond is set for each worker, so that by retirement it will be sufficient to pay a proportion of the old system's benefits equal to the proportion of lifetime taxes the worker paid under the old system.

Workers were given the choice of moving to the new private system or remaining in the existing government-run social security system. Within 18 months, more than 90 percent of workers chose the new private system.

After 17 years of operation, Chile's experiment has proven itself. Benefits in the new private system already are 50 to 100 percent higher than they were in the old state-run system. Yet the required payments for the private system are about 50 percent less. The resources administered by the private pension funds amounted to $30 billion, or about 43 percent of gross domestic product as of 1997. Because it has improved the functioning of both the capital and the labor markets, pension privatization has been one of the key reforms that has pushed Chile's economic growth rate up from the historical rate of 3 percent a year to 7 percent, on average, during the past 12 years. The Chilean savings rate has increased to 27 percent of GDP, and the unemployment rate has decreased to 5 percent since the reform was undertaken.

Moreover, as a result of the earnings and investments rapidly accumulating in private retirement accounts, in less than 10 years the average Chilean worker will have more retirement savings than the average American worker, even though the average American worker earns seven times the annual income of the average Chilean worker. Chilean labor union leader Eduardo Aguilera has said, "The bottom line is that the private pension system has been an enormous advancement for the Chilean workers." Like many labor union leaders in Chile, Aguilera was initially opposed to the reform but is now an enthusiastic supporter.

Chile's experience has been such a great economic and political success that other countries are considering and adopting similar reforms. Six other nations in Latin America have already adopted such reform: Argentina, Peru, Colombia, Bolivia, Mexico, and El Salvador. Less well-known is that Great Britain began a private option for social security almost 20 years ago, and almost 80 percent of British workers have now opted out of a portion of the government-run system. Australia has also quietly adopted a privately invested system for its workers within the past few years. Similar reforms are under active government consideration in the rest of Latin America, Eastern Europe, Western Europe, and even China.

In 1994 the World Bank examined this trend in its 400-page report, *Averting the Old-Age Crisis*. The report concluded that the Chilean reform was a great success. It advocated similar reforms for all countries to address the worldwide crisis in social security systems and to stimulate economic growth.

The Revolution Comes to America

The worldwide revolution in social security has finally come to America as well. If you like the idea of a private system for Social Security, you are not alone. Major national polls now show that Americans overwhelmingly support the idea. Every day, more and more leaders from across the political spectrum announce their support.

America actually has some limited experience with a privatized social security system. At about the same time that Chile adopted its reform in 1981, a quiet revolution was going on in south Texas. Three counties near Galveston, Texas, switched from Social Security to a privately invested system for their own county government workers. (At that time, the law allowed state and local government workers to make such a choice. The law has been changed to prohibit further switches.)

The system for those county workers operates much like the Chilean system. The workers pay into private investment accounts in place of Social Security. Private investment companies invest the funds in stocks, bonds, and other instruments. In retirement, the accumulated funds are used to pay for an annuity guaranteeing workers a specified monthly income for the rest of their lives. The plan also includes private life insurance and private disability insurance substituting for the survivors' and disability benefits of Social Security. Today, those who retire after 20 years of work under that system will receive three to four times the benefits that Social Security would pay them. Not surprisingly, survivors' and disability benefits are higher too.

But what of the rest of America? Will John, Jane, and the rest of us have the opportunity to privately invest our Social Security taxes?

Adoption of such a system for all American workers is now gaining support across the country. Early in 1996, one of the top economists in the country, Harvard professor Martin Feldstein, who is also president of the National Bureau of Economic Research, called for just such reform in an address to the American Economics Association. Feldstein estimated that the net gain to America from switching to a private system would be *$10 trillion* to *$20 trillion*! That would be about two to three times the annual output of our entire economy. Such reform has also been endorsed by Nobel Prize-winning economists Gary Becker, James Buchanan, and Milton Friedman, as well as former American Economics Association president Arnold Harberger, among others.

Long-time anti-poverty activist Sam Beard is now popularizing the benefits of such reform with his book, *Restoring Hope in America*. A former aide to Sen. Robert Kennedy, Beard has dedicated his life to bringing economic growth to the inner city, most notably through his National Development Council. In his book, Beard shows that a privately invested system would allow the middle class to retire as millionaires. Most important, he argues that giving lower-income workers control over some capital through such a private system is the key to breaking the cycle of poverty in inner-city areas. Beard is now on a long-term national campaign that conducts regular conferences in inner-city areas across the country to explain and promote the idea among the nation's poor and minorities, whom he believes will be helped the most.

Marshall Carter and William Shipman of State Street Global Advisors, the largest pension investment management firm in the country, have also written a new book on the subject, *Promises to Keep: Saving Social Security's Dream*. Drawing on their years of experience in the investment field, they show that a privately invested system would give workers three to six times the benefits promised by Social Security. That includes low-income workers as well as others. Economist Robert Genetski reached the same conclusion in his book, *A Nation of Millionaires*.

Late in 1996, the usually quiet Advisory Council on Social Security surprised the country. The president appoints council members every five years to review Social Security, identify problems, and recommend changes. Usually, the council insists everything is fine with Social Security and recommends only minor changes.

But this council, appointed by President Clinton, was different. Its members all agreed that some sort of new, invested system was necessary, for all the reasons we have discussed. And 5 of 13 council members supported allowing workers an option to choose a privately invested system for approximately half of their Social Security taxes.

Early in 1997 the Oregon state legislature passed a resolution calling on Congress to enact legislation to allow the state to adopt its own privately invested plan in place of Social Security for all workers in the state. The resolution is based on a precedent in federal welfare programs, where states could ask the federal government for a waiver to adopt their own welfare experiments and reforms. Highly successful innovations have resulted from that waiver process. Oregon is now asking Congress to adopt a similar waiver system for Social Security, so states can try their own Social Security reforms.

In 1995 the Cato Institute launched what has become a highly successful project to advance a privately invested, alternative system to Social Security. Headed by José Piñera, architect of the successful Chilean system, its Advisory Committee includes top economists Becker, Harberger, and Shipman, as well as Dorcas Hardy, a former commissioner of Social Security, and Tim Penny, a former Democratic congressman. Americans for Tax Reform, an influential grassroots taxpayer organization, has also recently launched a campaign for a private option for Social Security. The national Jaycees are also conducting informative seminars across the country to educate young people on this issue.

Those activities are building on powerfully favorable grassroots opinion. A 1994 Luntz Research poll found that 82 percent of adults under age 35 supported the idea ''of directing a portion of their Social Security taxes into a personal retirement account like an IRA which could be kept at any financial institution they would like, and receiving less in Social Security benefits from the government.'' A 1995 Luntz poll of all adults, conducted for the seniors' organization 60 Plus, found the public supporting such an option by 77 to 14 percent. In 1996 Bill McInturff of Public Opinion Strategies, perhaps the leading polling firm for political campaigns, conducted a nationwide poll for the Cato Institute that found the public favoring the idea by 68 to 11 percent. Most recently, a poll for the Democratic Leadership Council, conducted by White House pollster Mark Penn, found that 73 percent of Democrats want to be able to privately invest all or part of their Social Security taxes.

Politicians are responding to the shift in public opinion. Reps. Jim Kolbe (R-Ariz.) and Charles Stenholm (D-Tex.) have launched a bipartisan caucus group in the House of Representatives to promote discussion of Social Security reform, including privatization. Approximately 80 members from both parties have joined. Among those developing specific legislation are Sens. Phil Gramm (R-Tex.), Rick Santorum (R-Penn.), Rod Grams (R-Minn.), Robert Kerrey (D-Neb.), Daniel Patrick Moynihan (D-N.Y.), and Judd Gregg (R-N.H.). In the House, legislation has been introduced by Reps. Nick Smith (R-Mich.), Mark Sanford Jr. (R-S.C.), and John Porter (R-Ill.).

Recently, Alan Greenspan warned that Social Security reform must come ''sooner rather than later'' and suggested that privatization was a viable solution to the system's problems.

Finally, and perhaps most important, President Clinton has now called for a national debate on Social Security reform and urged Congress to enact Social Security legislation by 1999. In announcing his call for Social Security reform, the president said Americans should be ''open to new ideas, not be hidebound and believe that we can see the future through the prism of the past.''

If Americans take that advice to heart, they may soon have the chance to join the rest of the world in moving to a new and better social security system.

6.
Common Sense

Still, Jane wondered, would it be possible to develop a privately invested system that would work for her and John? They were inexperienced investors and knew very little about the stock market. Jane also wanted to be sure that any new system would provide good opportunities for her young children, Jack and Jill. At the same time, she wanted to be sure that changes would not hurt her retired father, George, who lived solely off his Social Security benefits.

A Plan for America

There are many ways a reform plan could be designed to offer workers a private alternative to Social Security.[1] Here is one example:

Workers would be allowed the freedom to choose to provide for their retirement, survivors', and disability benefits through a private investment account, like an IRA or 401(k) plan, in place of Social Security. Workers currently pay 12.4

---

[1] In an ideal world, Social Security would be voluntary. People should be free to choose the best way to provide for their own retirement. The authors believe that most people are prudent and would provide for their retirement needs. Those who didn't could be cared for through private charity. This is the only retirement system that is ultimately compatible with human liberty. However, the authors understand the political reality that any alternative to Social Security will provide for a mandatory system of savings.

percent of their wages in Social Security payroll taxes (with payments split equally between the employer and employee). Because the return on private investment is so much higher than Social Security can provide, however, the worker can pay less into the private plan and still receive much higher benefits than those promised by Social Security.

If the worker chose the private plan, the worker and employer might be required to pay only 5 percent each into that plan, a total of 10 percent instead of the 12.4 percent paid today. For a few years, the remaining 2.4 percent could still be paid to Social Security to help pay the continuing benefits for current retirees. But after a strictly limited period, not more than 10 years at most, that extra portion of the payroll tax could be eliminated for those choosing the private option, resulting in a 20 percent tax cut for those workers and their employers.

Part of the funds paid into the private plan could be used to purchase private life and disability insurance covering at least the same survivors' and disability benefits that Social Security now provides. The rest of the funds could be saved and invested over the years to pay for the worker's retirement benefits. Workers could choose from among a broad range of government-approved and government-regulated investment management companies to handle their investments. Those would include major stock brokerage firms, such as Merrill Lynch; mutual funds, such as Fidelity Investments; banks; and insurance companies.

The investment company the worker chose would then select stocks, bonds, and other investments for the worker's account. As a result, the worker would not need to be an experienced investor, but simply would need to pick an investment company with a proven reputation. That system has worked well for even the most unsophisticated workers in Latin America, where countries have already adopted such a private option. Workers could switch investment companies on short notice.

The private retirement accounts would be kept separate from all other finances and activities of the investment companies. If an investment company failed, the government would take possession of its retirement accounts and investments and transfer them to other investment companies chosen by each worker. Workers would not lose their savings.

The same restrictions that apply to IRAs today would apply to investments in the private retirement accounts. Workers would not be allowed to withdraw funds from the accounts before retirement, for example. They would have broad scope in choosing investments to earn the highest reliable returns, but highly risky and speculative investments would be excluded.

At retirement, workers could use their accumulated retirement account funds to purchase an annuity from an insurance company or bank. That annuity would pay benefits for the rest of the worker's life. If desired, the annuity could be designed to continue to pay benefits for the life of a surviving spouse after the worker died.

Alternatively, workers could keep their accumulated funds and live off the annual investment returns and regular, periodic withdrawals. They could then conserve their saved funds and leave them to their children or other heirs. Regulations would limit withdrawals so the retiree couldn't use up all the funds early and then be left without retirement support.

The government would guarantee all retirees in the private system a minimum benefit. If a retiree's retirement account funds were not enough to pay at least that minimum benefit, then the government would pay supplemental benefits to the retiree to ensure that total benefits would reach at least that minimum level.

With the high benefits of the private system, that minimum benefit could be set at a generous level close to the average benefit from Social Security. The high private benefits would leave few, if any, in need of minimum supplemental benefits. With the private system expected to pay three or more times Social Security with just average investment performance, even those whose investments do poorly for whatever reason would likely still have more than the average benefit under Social Security.

Workers would be free to choose their own retirement age and could retire early if their accumulated retirement account funds were sufficient to provide a specified standard of benefits throughout retirement. That could be achieved with above-average investment performance, or by voluntary extra payments into the retirement account during working years. Of course, retiring earlier would mean lower benefits.

The government would provide bonds to workers who had already paid taxes into the old Social Security system and who chose to switch to the new private system. Those bonds would be held in their retirement accounts as repayment for the taxes they paid into Social Security. The bonds would draw interest over the years and in retirement would pay a proportion of Social Security benefits equal to the proportion of lifetime taxes the worker had paid into the old Social Security system.

For example, if a worker had paid into the old Social Security system for half his career and then switched to the private system, the recognition bonds would pay the retired worker half the benefits of Social Security, in addition to the benefits he would receive from the private system. If the worker had paid into Social Security for one-fourth of his career, the bonds would pay him one-fourth of Social Security benefits.

Workers would have the freedom to choose to stay in the current Social Security system if they preferred. Those who did would still be free to switch to the private system at any point later in their careers. Of course, each year they waited, they would lose some of the higher benefits of the private system.

For those already retired on Social Security, no change would occur. They would continue to receive their current benefits, which would be financed in part by the portion of Social Security payroll taxes that those who opted for the private system would continue to pay for a few years. The government could raise more money for those benefits by cutting other government spending, selling government bonds, and selling unneeded government assets. The new savings and investment in the private system would also generate huge additional tax revenues. Those sources of funds would be more than sufficient to pay the benefits promised to today's retirees, as they have in the other countries that have adopted such reform.

Of course that is not the only way a private social security system might be designed. Many other plans and proposals are being debated. But that is one example of how a system based on individually owned, privately invested accounts might work in America.

Freedom and Prosperity

A privately invested Social Security plan would benefit the American people enormously.

Solving Social Security's Long-Term Financing Problems

The reform would eliminate Social Security's long-term financing crisis. As young workers chose the new privately invested system, the issue of how to pay for their benefits through the bankrupt Social Security system would no longer be relevant. In a private system, all future benefits would be fully funded by private savings and investments, so no long-term financing crisis would exist. The money to finance retirement benefits would always be on hand in workers' personal accounts.

A Better Deal for Today's Workers

A private system would provide workers with much higher returns and benefits. Couples consisting of two average-income workers would reach retirement with more than $1 million in retirement savings (in today's dollars after adjusting for inflation). Such a fund would pay at least three times as much as Social Security would pay. They could live off the interest, which would still pay higher benefits than Social Security, and leave the $1 million to their children.

Everyone would receive much higher benefits through the private system with just average investment returns—low-income workers, high-income workers, married couples, single people, one-earner couples, two-earner couples, families with children, families without children, blacks, whites, Hispanics, and indeed all Americans.

Higher Savings and Economic Growth

The private system would likely produce a large increase in national savings, with hundreds of billions of dollars invested in individual retirement accounts each year. Those investments, in turn, would substantially increase national investment, productivity, wages, jobs, and overall economic growth. The effective payroll tax cut resulting from the private option would also boost employment and economic growth. Harvard economist Martin Feldstein estimates that privatizing Social Security would permanently raise U.S. GDP by 5 percent.

Fairness

The private system would be the most fair because it would offer to everyone the same opportunities to invest. Indeed, lower-income workers, who are most in need of the higher returns and benefits of a private system, would benefit the most. A private system offers them their only chance to accumulate savings for their retirement and to leave to their children. Blacks and other minorities who live fewer years in retirement would be able to leave their accumulated funds to their children instead of losing them as many now do under Social Security. Lower-income workers are also most in need of the increased jobs, wages, and economic growth that would likely result from Social Security privatization.

They are also the most vulnerable to the long-term crisis the current system faces. They cannot afford higher taxes now or reduced benefits in retirement.

Freedom of Choice and Control

A private system would allow American workers much greater freedom of choice and control over their own incomes and financial futures. Through a privately invested system, the one-eighth of their incomes that now goes to Social Security would grow to a huge amount that would be under their direct, personal control. The investment earning power of average- and even modest-income earners would bear fruit. The effect of compound interest on even average investment returns would make average-income couples literal millionaires by retirement. Those funds would do more to help the family than any other economic reform.

Finally, all of this would be accomplished without harming today's retirees. Neither their benefits nor their overall program would change.

Other countries are recognizing those enormous benefits and adopting reforms for their workers. What about the American people? Are they going to be left behind by a political system gridlocked by special-interest groups that ultimately represent only themselves? If we cannot change, then in a couple of generations, workers in South America, East Asia, and Eastern Europe will be retiring as millionaires while Americans will still be paying ever higher taxes for dwindling Social Security benefits.

In the end, America's workers are the ones who can change America's Social Security system. If every John and Jane, Tom and LaShawn, and Mary and Paul in America spread the word to their neighbors, organized local groups, and expressed their views to their congressional representatives, then we could develop a new system that would benefit both today's workers and future generations.

It's up to you.

About the Authors

Michael D. Tanner is director of health and welfare studies with the Cato Institute in Washington, D.C., and director of Cato's Project on Social Security Privatization. Before joining Cato in 1993, he served as director of research for the Georgia Public Policy Foundation in Atlanta. He also spent five years as legislative director with the American Legislative Exchange Council, where he specialized in health and welfare issues.

Tanner is the author of seven books on health and welfare reform, as well as numerous studies on health, welfare, and Social Security issues. His work has appeared in most major newspapers including the *Washington Post, Wall Street Journal, Baltimore Sun, Washington Times, Indianapolis Star, Cleveland Plain Dealer, Detroit News,* and *USA Today.* A frequent media guest, he has appeared on *ABC World News Tonight, CBS Evening News, PBS News Hour, NBC Dateline,* and *Good Morning America,* among other programs.

Peter J. Ferrara is the general counsel and chief economist for Americans for Tax Reform, the nation's largest grassroots advocacy group, and an associate policy analyst with the Cato Institute. Previously he served in a variety of positions with the Cato Institute, the Heritage Foundation, and the National Center for Policy Analysis. He served as associate deputy attorney general of the United States from 1992 to 1993 and served in the Reagan Administration from 1981 to 1983.

Considered one of the foremost experts on Social Security privatization, Ferrara has published numerous books and articles, including *Social Security: The Inherent Contradiction.* His writing has appeared in such publications as the *Wall Street Journal, Washington Times, National Review,* and *Reader's Digest.* He is the coauthor of *A New Deal for Social Security.*

Additional Reading

For additional information on this important issue, you may want to read the authors' more extensive study,

Peter Ferrara and Michael Tanner, *A New Deal for Social Security* (Washington: Cato Institute, 1998).

You may also want to read

Sam Beard, *Restoring Hope in America: The Social Security Solution* (San Francisco: Institute for Contemporary Studies, 1996).

Marshall Carter and William Shipman, *Promises to Keep: Saving Social Security's Dream* (Washington: Regnery, 1996).

Peter Ferrara, *Social Security: The Inherent Contradiction* (Washington: Cato Institute, 1980).

Dorcas Hardy and C. Colburn Hardy, *Social Insecurity: The Crisis in America's Social Security System and How to Plan Now for Your Own Financial Survival* (New York: Villard Books, 1996).

E. J. Myers, *Let's Get Rid of Social Security: How Americans Can Take Charge of their Own Future* (Amherst, N.Y.: Prometheus Books, 1996).

A. Haeworth Robertson, *The Big Lie: What Every Baby Boomer Should Know about Social Security and Medicare* (Washington: Retirement Policy Institute, 1997).

Cato Institute

Founded in 1977, the Cato Institute is a public policy research foundation dedicated to broadening the parameters of policy debate to allow consideration of more options that are consistent with the traditional American principles of limited government, individual liberty, and peace. To that end, the Institute strives to achieve greater involvement of the intelligent, concerned lay public in questions of policy and the proper role of government.

The Institute is named for *Cato's Letters*, libertarian pamphlets that were widely read in the American Colonies in the early 18th century and played a major role in laying the philosophical foundation for the American Revolution.

Despite the achievement of the nation's Founders, today virtually no aspect of life is free from government encroachment. A pervasive intolerance for individual rights is shown by government's arbitrary intrusions into private economic transactions and its disregard for civil liberties.

To counter that trend, the Cato Institute undertakes an extensive publications program that addresses the complete spectrum of policy issues. Books, monographs, and shorter studies are commissioned to examine the federal budget, Social Security, regulation, military spending, international trade, and myriad other issues. Major policy conferences are held throughout the year, from which papers are published thrice yearly in the *Cato Journal*. The Institute also publishes the quarterly magazine *Regulation*.

In order to maintain its independence, the Cato Institute accepts no government funding. Contributions are received from foundations, corporations, and individuals, and other revenue is generated from the sale of publications. The Institute is a nonprofit, tax-exempt, educational foundation under Section 501(c)3 of the Internal Revenue Code.

CATO INSTITUTE
1000 Massachusetts Ave., N.W.
Washington, D.C. 20001

How does Social Security compare with what you could earn from private investment? You can check it out for yourself. If you have access to the Internet, visit the Cato Institute's Social Security Web site at **www.socialsecurity.org.** In addition to articles and studies on Social Security privatization, this site contains an interactive calculator designed by the accounting firm of KPMG Peat Marwick. You can enter your personal data (age, income, etc.) and see what your future Social Security benefits would be and how they compare with what you could earn in a privately invested system.

SOCIAL SECURITY	BOND FUND	MIXED FUND	STOCK FUND
$13,818	$21,896	$40,566	$77,973

A 20-year-old could expect to receive much higher annual retirement benefits from a variety of privatization plans than from the current Social Security system.